Little People, **BIG DREAMS**®

TAYLOR SWIFT

Written by
Maria Isabel Sánchez Vegara

Illustrated by
Borghild Fallberg

Frances Lincoln
Children's Books

On a farm in Pennsylvania, USA, surrounded by Christmas trees, lived a girl named Taylor. She believed in unicorns and fairy tales, but most of all she believed in the power of songs to tell stories and change the world.

Her grandmother was an opera singer, and her parents were also music lovers. One day, her mum and dad took her to a country-music concert. Taylor was moved by the sound and the way the artist shared her feelings through her songs.

I ♥ COUNTRY

WE ♥ LEANN RIMES

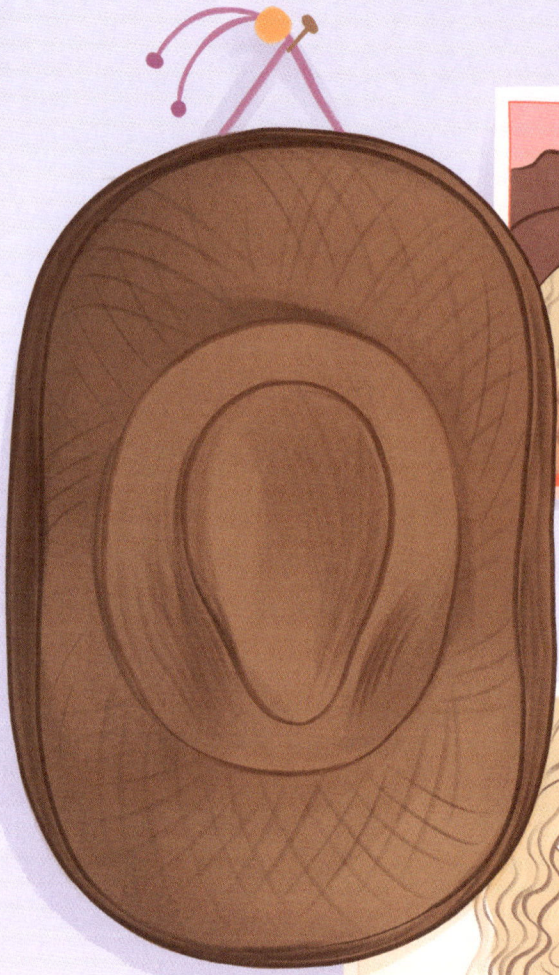

Soon she was dragging her parents to county fairs, festivals and karaoke contests, jumping on stage to sing whenever she had a chance. She also took singing and acting lessons and enjoyed performing in local musicals.

Yet school was a lonely place for Taylor. Most students didn't think country music was cool, and a few of them made fun of her cowboy boots. But even though people weren't always there for her, music was, and she kept pursuing her dream.

COUNTRY MUSIC STUDIO

DEMOS

Taylor was eleven when she sang and recorded cover versions of her most beloved songs, pouring her heart into every tune. She took her demo to Nashville, the home of country music.

There, she realized that to stand out she needed
to find her own voice.

Back home, Taylor learnt to play the guitar and began writing songs inspired by her own life. The first was called 'Lucky You'. It was about a little girl with a big heart. Soon her head was full of more rhymes, melodies and lyrics.

After being spotted at one of her gigs, Taylor recorded her first album for a record label. She became the youngest person ever to write and perform a number-one country song. It was honest, smart and funny. Everyone loved it!

By her twentieth birthday, she had released her second album, *Fearless*. It won her four Grammys – the most prestigious music awards. Taylor's parents were so proud. Her journey to becoming a megastar had just begun!

Taylor continued to grow up alongside her fans.
She loved to include hidden messages for them
in her lyrics and music videos.

Before the release of her fifth album, *1989*, she invited groups of eighty-nine of them to listen to it and eat cookies at her home.

reput

But living in the spotlight can be tough. There was always someone ready to criticize her no matter what she did. It took time for Taylor to learn that the only approval she needed was her own, and once she did, she stood up stronger than ever.

She made pop, rock, electronic and folk music.
Yet she also found time to tour the world, direct her own
music videos, speak up for what she believed in and care for
Meredith Grey, Olivia Benson and Benjamin Button, her cats.

Almost twenty years after writing her first song, Taylor made history as the first artist to hold all top-ten spots in the biggest US music chart. But while her list of records and awards kept growing, being a kind person was still her main goal.

And Taylor, the little girl who believed in fairy tales, keeps achieving even her wildest dreams! She is one of the greatest artists of her generation and a friend to millions of fans who feel her music tells the story of their own lives.

TAYLOR SWIFT

(Born 1989)

2007

2009

Taylor Alison Swift was born in Pennsylvania, USA, into a music-loving family. She was named after the singer-songwriter James Taylor, who she performed with years later. As a child she loved running around the Christmas-tree farm where she lived. After attending a LeAnn Rimes concert, Taylor found her passion for music, and aged eleven she self-recorded a demo of cover songs and delivered her CDs to record labels. Although she wasn't offered a deal, she was encouraged to keep trying. Soon after she learnt to play the guitar and started writing songs. Taylor fell in love with crafting lyrics, and her teachers even found them scribbled inside her exercise books. At fourteen years old she was spotted while gigging at the Bluebird Cafe in Nashville, Tennessee, and later

2016   2023

signed with Big Machine Records. Six studio albums followed, including
the hit singles 'Love Story', 'Shake it Off' and 'Bad Blood'. When her
masters were sold without her permission, Taylor decided to take back
ownership of her art and re-record all six albums with a new record label,
adding unreleased songs. In her 2020 documentary, *Miss Americana*,
she spoke about learning to care for her mental health and using her
voice for good. Taylor passionately believes in dignity for all people,
'no matter their skin colour, gender or who they love'. In 2022,
after releasing her tenth album, she announced The Eras Tour. Each show
celebrated her musical journey, enchanting 'Swifties' across the world.
Taylor's story reminds us to be fearless in the pursuit of our dreams.

Want to find out more about **Taylor Swift**?

Have a read of this great book:

Be More Taylor Swift: Fearless Advice on Following Your Dreams and Finding Your Voice by DK.

With help from an adult, you can listen to Taylor's songs online.

Text © 2024 Maria Isabel Sánchez Vegara. Illustrations © 2024 Borghild Fallberg.
Original idea of the series by Maria Isabel Sánchez Vegara, published by Alba Editorial, s.l.u
"Little People, BIG DREAMS" and "Pequeña & Grande" are trademarks of
Alba Editorial s.l.u. and/or Beautifool Couple S.L.
First Published in the UK in 2024 by Frances Lincoln Children's Books, an imprint of The Quarto Group.
1 Triptych Place, London, SE1 9SH, United Kingdom. T 020 7700 6700 www.Quarto.com
All rights reserved.

A catalogue record for this book is available from the British Library.
ISBN 978-0-7112-9508-7
Set in Futura BT.
Published by Peter Marley · Designed by Sasha Moxon
Commissioned by Lucy Menzies · Edited by Molly Mead
Production by Nikki Ingram

Manufactured in Bosnia and Herzegovina
7 9 8

Photographic acknowledgements (pages 28-29, from left to right): 1. 4/5/2007 Photo by Krissy Krummenacker 200700708 Country singer Taylor Swift, originally from Wyomissing, sings the national anthem Thursday, April 5, 2007, before the Reading Phillies opening game against the Harrisburg Senators at FirstEnergy Stadium © Krissy Krummenacker/MediaNews Group/Reading Eagle via Getty Images. 2. Taylor Swift Fearless Tour: Musician Taylor Swift prepares backstage at Madison Square Garden on August 27, 2009 in New York City © Larry Busacca via Getty Images for Erickson Public. 3. Singer Taylor Swift, winner of the awards for Album of the Year and Best Pop Album for '1989' and Best Music Video for 'Bad Blood,' poses in the press room during The 58TH GRAMMY Awards at Staples Center on February 15, 2016 in Los Angeles, California © Dan MacMedan/WireImage via Getty Images. 4. Taylor Swift performs onstage during the "Taylor Swift | The Eras Tour" at Foro Sol on August 24, 2023 in Mexico City, Mexico © Hector Vivas/TAS23 via Getty Images for TAS Rights Management.

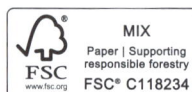

Collect the *Little People*, **BIG DREAMS**® series:

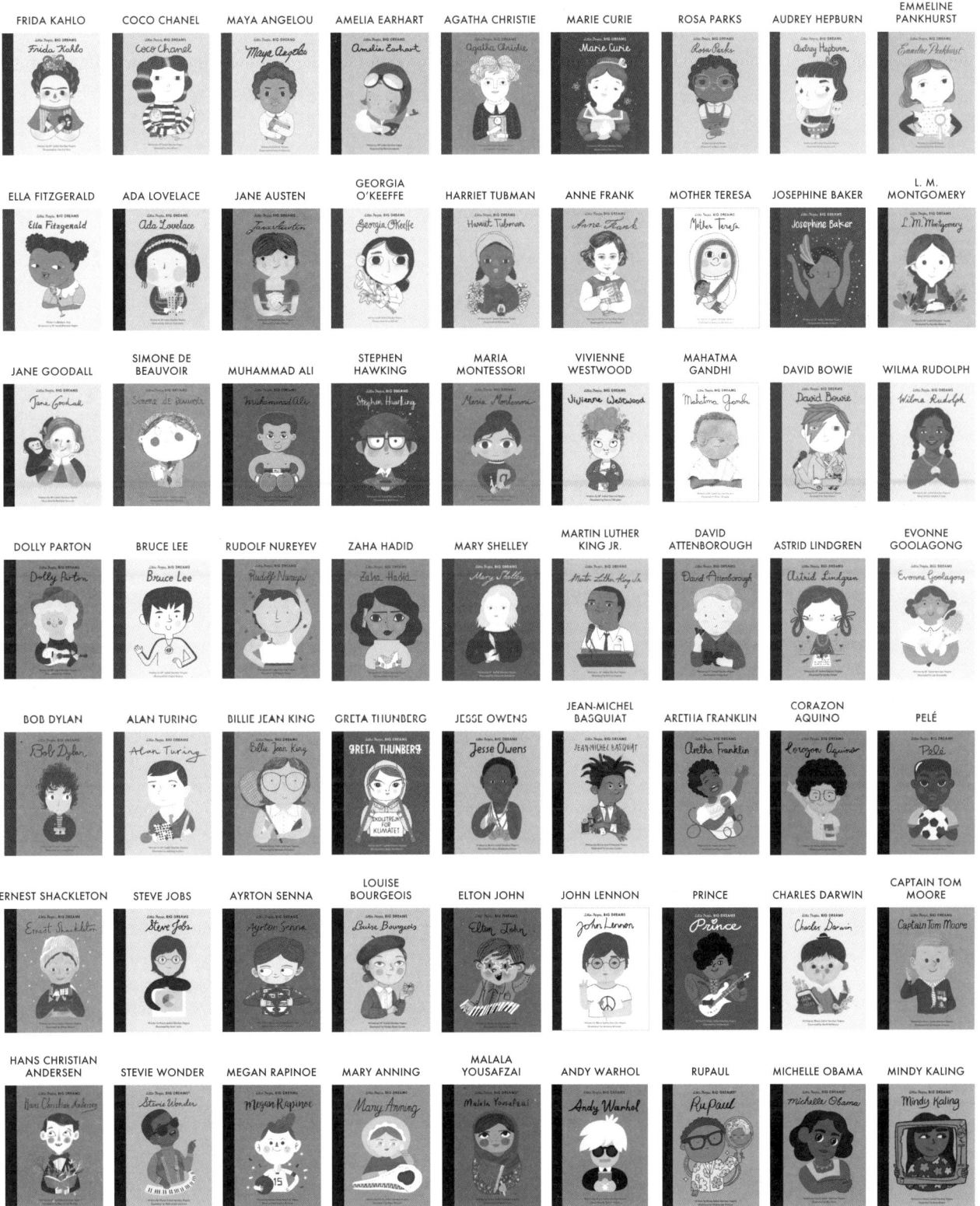

FRIDA KAHLO	COCO CHANEL	MAYA ANGELOU	AMELIA EARHART	AGATHA CHRISTIE	MARIE CURIE	ROSA PARKS	AUDREY HEPBURN	EMMELINE PANKHURST

ELLA FITZGERALD	ADA LOVELACE	JANE AUSTEN	GEORGIA O'KEEFFE	HARRIET TUBMAN	ANNE FRANK	MOTHER TERESA	JOSEPHINE BAKER	L. M. MONTGOMERY

JANE GOODALL	SIMONE DE BEAUVOIR	MUHAMMAD ALI	STEPHEN HAWKING	MARIA MONTESSORI	VIVIENNE WESTWOOD	MAHATMA GANDHI	DAVID BOWIE	WILMA RUDOLPH

DOLLY PARTON	BRUCE LEE	RUDOLF NUREYEV	ZAHA HADID	MARY SHELLEY	MARTIN LUTHER KING JR.	DAVID ATTENBOROUGH	ASTRID LINDGREN	EVONNE GOOLAGONG

BOB DYLAN	ALAN TURING	BILLIE JEAN KING	GRETA THUNBERG	JESSE OWENS	JEAN-MICHEL BASQUIAT	ARETHA FRANKLIN	CORAZON AQUINO	PELÉ

ERNEST SHACKLETON	STEVE JOBS	AYRTON SENNA	LOUISE BOURGEOIS	ELTON JOHN	JOHN LENNON	PRINCE	CHARLES DARWIN	CAPTAIN TOM MOORE

HANS CHRISTIAN ANDERSEN	STEVIE WONDER	MEGAN RAPINOE	MARY ANNING	MALALA YOUSAFZAI	ANDY WARHOL	RUPAUL	MICHELLE OBAMA	MINDY KALING

IRIS APFEL   ROSALIND FRANKLIN   RUTH BADER GINSBURG   MARILYN MONROE   KAMALA HARRIS   ALBERT EINSTEIN   CHARLES DICKENS   YOKO ONO   MICHAEL JORDAN

NELSON MANDELA   PABLO PICASSO   AMANDA GORMAN   GLORIA STEINEM   FLORENCE NIGHTINGALE   HARRY HOUDINI   J.R.R. TOLKIEN   ELVIS PRESLEY   NEIL ARMSTRONG

ALEXANDER VON HUMBOLDT   NIKOLA TESLA   WILMA MANKILLER   MARCUS RASHFORD   LAVERNE COX   MAE JEMISON   DWAYNE JOHNSON   HELEN KELLER   ANNA PAVLOVA

QUEEN ELIZABETH   TERRY FOX   HEDY LAMARR   SHAKIRA   FREDDIE MERCURY   LEWIS HAMILTON   LOUIS PASTEUR   PRINCESS DIANA   DAVID HOCKNEY

VANESSA NAKATE   OLIVE MORRIS   KING CHARLES   MOZART   STEVE IRWIN   JÜRGEN KLOPP   LEO MESSI   SALLY RIDE   TENZING NORGAY

LENNY HENRY   KYLIE MINOGUE   BEYONCÉ   TAYLOR SWIFT   RAFA NADAL

NANA BAJWA

Scan the QR code for free activity
sheets, teachers' notes and more
information about the series at
www.littlepeoplebigdreams.com